THE TWO-PART CHRISTIAN GOSPEL

Walking in the Way of Christ & the Apostles
Study Guide Series
Part 1, Book 6
A 9-Session Study

Peter Briggs

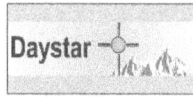

ISBN: 9781947642065

Daystar

Published by:
Daystar Institute / NM, Inc.
P.O. Box 50567
Albuquerque, NM 87181
http://www.daystarinstitutenm.us/

Distributed in Africa by:
Daystar Institute / Africa
Kampala, Uganda
http://www.daystarinstituteafrica.org/

Table of Contents

Foreword

Jesus Christ, in His three-year ministry with His twelve disciples, modeled the method for teaching disciples to walk in His way.

The Walking in the Way (WitW) Study Guide Series attempts to model Christ's method of teaching by utilizing a holistic approach designed to challenge students to apply biblical principles to their lives and ministries. Our aim is to equip disciples of Jesus to "walk in him, rooted and built up in him and established in the faith, just as you were taught, abounding in thanksgiving." Colossians 2:6,7. Thus, we emphasize wholehearted discipleship, practical Christian theology, and a biblical world view.

We have prayerfully designed the WitW study materials to equip you with the tools and concepts needed to achieve this goal. May the word of God dwell in our hearts richly through faith by studying it, reflecting upon it, and allowing it to penetrate the deepest recesses of our souls. By this means, we bring our hearts and minds into alignment with God's heart and mind.

How to Use this Study Guide

Although this Bible study may be done independently, we strongly recommend using it in a group setting. Study each session prayerfully and reflect deeply on the included passages of Scripture as part of your daily devotional time with God. Establish a journal in which you record your answers to questions, as well as your reflections and notes.

If you are participating in a group study, be prepared to interact with your leader and group members. This includes sharing insights and practical lessons God is teaching you personally.

Read the questions and associated Scripture passages aloud and stick to the Bible as your sole authority for answers given. At the end of each discussion session, take time to pray for group member needs; then hold one another accountable for putting the lessons learned into practice.

Upon completion of one book, move on to the next book in the series. In parallel, begin sharing the WitW teaching with family members, work associates, and others in your circle of influence.

Leaders may use their discretion as to how much material to cover in any given discussion session. We also encourage Bible study teachers and leaders to read the associated WitW Theological Handbook or Theological Reader in order to gain a better understanding of the material presented in this booklet. Our resources are listed in the back of this study guide and are available on Amazon.com.

Introduction to Book 6

Everyone welcomes good news. We rejoice at a wedding, the birth of a baby, a promotion at work, or the salvation of a loved one.

Yet we are often reluctant to share the best news of all – that of the rescue and deliverance from evil, sin, and death that Jesus Christ procured for us at horrendous cost to Himself.

It is our prayer that our studies in this book will help you grasp the breadth, depth, and richness of the Christian gospel as a complete solution to the problem of evil, sin, and death, and that it will equip you with the knowledge and confidence to be able to share your faith boldly and lovingly with those in your circle of influence.

Book 6 Goals

To understand the two aspects of the Christian gospel: namely, the **gospel of the kingdom of God**, which is revealed through the Synoptic Gospels and the Book of Acts; and **the gospel of God**, which is introduced in the Gospel of John and discussed and developed in the Pauline Epistles.

To be able to clearly explain the Christian gospel to another person.

To understand the two primary corruptions of the Christian gospel and why they are dangerous.

To practice the Christian gospel in our lives and ministries.

Our desire is that every disciple of Jesus Christ be firmly rooted, built up, and established in his faith in accordance with Colossians 2:6-7. We have prayerfully designed the WitW study materials to equip you with the tools and concepts needed to achieve this goal. May the Word of God dwell in our hearts richly through faith by studying it, reflecting upon it, and allowing it to penetrate into the deepest recesses of our souls. By this means, we bring our hearts and minds into alignment with God's heart and mind.

As you begin each lesson, pray that God would open your heart to the study of His Word, that He would speak to you through His Word, and that He would cause His Holy Spirit to use the Word of God to break up the fallow ground in your heart. This study is not about learning a lot of facts – it is about living out the truth of Scripture in order to glorify God and impact others for the advancement of Christ's kingdom.

Notes & Reflections

Formulate a statement of your personal goals and objectives for this study of the two-part Christian gospel. Also, make note of any additional insights or comments as you begin this study.

Session 1. The Gospel Family of Motifs – Part One

Good news is always welcome, regardless of whether it is seemingly inconsequential, like a word from an old friend, or something momentous like an engagement, a wedding, the birth of a child, or a promotion at work. But the best news of all is the Christian gospel by means of which we are offered an eternal relationship with Jesus Christ, and, through Him, with God the Father.

To introduce our exploration of the two-part Christian gospel, let us turn to the writings of the apostles in the Christian Scriptures.

Read John 1:1-4 & 12-14, John 3:16, Acts 4:12, 1 Corinthians 15:1-11 & 21-22, Titus 2:11-14, and Titus 3:4-7.

Q 1.   Based upon the testimonies of the apostles John, Luke, and Paul recorded in the above passages, summarize the content of the Christian gospel.

These verses suggest that the gospel is supernatural, personal, and universally accessible. It is both life-giving and life-transforming. While these aspects of the gospel are amazing, the gospel is so much more.

In this study guide we will endeavor to unfold the richness and beauty of the Christian gospel by noting the origin and tracing the trajectory of a number of the fourteen integrative motifs introduced in Book 5. We designate the particular set of motifs which we will consider in this study guide as **the gospel family of motifs**. Principle in this set of motifs is, of course, The Gospel motif itself. The family also includes the other motifs that intersect with The Gospel motif in important ways. By means of our discussions in the six sessions of this book, we will endeavor to weave a tapestry from a number of strands that reveals the glory of the Christian gospel; that is, how rich, complex, and intricate it is, including its background in the book of Genesis.

We will then consider the two-part Christian gospel: namely, the **gospel of the kingdom of God**, which is revealed through the Synoptic Gospels and the Book of Acts; and the **gospel of God**, which is introduced in the Gospel of John and discussed and developed in the Pauline Epistles. By means of our exploration of the gospel family of motifs, we will discover that the gospel of God is actually rooted in the Protoevangelium of Genesis 3:15, and that the gospel of the kingdom of God is rooted in the covenant which Yahweh Elohim enacted with the nation of Israel at Mt. Sinai through the ministry of Moses. The focal passage which defines the source or origin of the gospel of the kingdom of God is Exodus 19:3-6.

The Fourteen Integrative Motifs

Following is the complete list of the fourteen integrative motifs upon which we touched in Book 5:

1. The Name of God

2. The Temple

3. The Sabbath

4. The Imago Dei

5. The Marriage Metaphor

6. The Invasion of Evil, Sin, and Death

7. The Seed of the Woman

8. Acceptable Sacrifice

9. The City of Man Versus the Kingdom of God

10. The People of the New Way

11. The Gospel

12. Sovereign Election and Human Responsibility

13. The Prototype

14. The Covenant of Conditional Blessing

Q 2.   For each of the motifs listed above, write a brief definition. Identify the motifs which intersect with and contribute to our understanding of The Gospel motif. In the space below, summarize each important intersection that you have been able to identify.

The Glory of the Christian Gospel

Because of the richness and complexity of the Christian gospel, it is important that we take time to carefully examine it. As we embark upon this examination, we are tempted to focus on the personal aspects of the Christian gospel; that is, the way in which it addresses the problem of personal sin in offering each of us redemption through the blood of Jesus Christ, God's Son. **However, its impact infinitely exceeds this!**

The Christian gospel brings about a cosmic resolution of the problem of evil, sin, and death. In fact, the infinite merit of Christ's redemptive work is such as to bring about a complete obliteration of all the effects of evil, sin, and death, and to restore the cosmos to God's original intent for it.

The Christ event – that is, the incarnation, birth, life and ministry, death, burial, and resurrection of Christ Jesus – is at the heart of the Christian gospel. The Christ event is that to which the Hebrew Scriptures look forward, and it is that which the Christian Scriptures record, describe, and discuss.

In your answer to Question (2) above, you might have noted that The Gospel motif intersects with The Invasion of Evil, Sin, and Death motif in that the curses Yahweh pronounced against man and Satan – that is, the effects of the Fall – are totally reversed and neutralized. It intersects with The Seed of the Woman motif in that Jesus is the promised deliverer. It intersects with The Acceptable Sacrifice motif in that Jesus Himself is the consummate acceptable sacrifice. It also intersects with The People of the New Way motif in that the blessings of the gospel are spread to all peoples and nations through the seed of Abraham. According to The Prototype motif, the experiences of the nation of Israel in the Exodus and Conquest episodes foreshadow the application of the gospel to the life of the individual Christ-follower. Finally, The Gospel motif intersects with The Covenant of Conditional Blessing motif in that the blessings which God promises in the gospel are linked to our obedience.

The gospel, then, demonstrates God's infinite love, mercy, and grace whereby He decisively deals with the problem of evil, sin, and death through His Son, Jesus Christ our Lord. Through the infinite merit of Jesus' redemptive work, God is able to completely nullify all the effects of evil, sin, and death, not only in the lives of individual human beings, but throughout the cosmos and for all eternity. It is a gospel of love, reconciliation, and deliverance – and is available to all who wholeheartedly embrace it!

Worthy is the Lamb that was slain, and has released us from our sins by His blood, and has made us to be a kingdom of priests unto His God and Father, to receive power and riches and wisdom and might and honor and glory and blessing; to Him be the glory and the dominion forever and ever. Amen! [A doxology synthesized from passages in the book of Revelation]

Although the essence of the Christian gospel is so simple that even a child can understand and embrace it, it is also so rich and complex that a lifetime of study and reflection is insufficient to fully comprehend it.

The Original State of the Cosmos

To set the stage for our consideration of the gospel family of motifs, let us pay careful attention to God's assessment of His work of creation.

Read Genesis 1:1-31.

Q 3.   What was God's assessment of His work of creation as expressed in Genesis 1:31? Given the nature and character of God, what are the implications of this statement?

The biblical account in Genesis 1 and 2 describes a perfect creation, one with which God was completely satisfied. In fact, we find Him stating that "it was good" six times in the 1st chapter of Genesis. And, then, after the creation of mankind, He states that "it was very good."

He considered man to be the crowning glory of His creation.

Q 4.   How did the Fall episode recorded in the 3rd chapter of Genesis change the perfect cosmos that existed at the end of the 2nd chapter?

Because of one tragic decision by our ancestor Adam, mankind and his earthly environment became infected and corrupted by evil, sin, and death, and, therefore, the need for healing and restoration – a **BIG problem!**

In fact, the problem of evil, sin, and death is so huge that it is completely beyond the scope of any humanly devised resolution.

The *Protoevangelium*

The gospel of God is rooted in the *Protoevangelium*, which is the very first gospel proclamation in all of Scripture. It is found in Genesis 3:15 – the curse that Yahweh Elohim pronounced upon the serpent:

> **Genesis 3:15.** I will put enmity between you and the woman, and between your seed and her seed; He shall strike your head, and you shall strike His heel. [Adapted from the ESV]

Q 5. With which of the fourteen motifs listed above does this statement intersect and in what ways?

Besides containing the Protoevangelium, Genesis 3:15 is the seminal passage for The Seed of the Woman motif. We will presently engage in a brief discussion of that motif. However, before we do, and as a segue into that discussion, carefully read the following Scripture passages:

Read Matthew 13:24-30 & 36-43, Galatians 3:15-18, and the 12th chapter of Revelation.

The pronouncement of Genesis 3:15 is addressed primarily to the serpent, which represents Satan in the Fall episode. In this verse, the Hebrew word translated "seed" or "offspring" is *zera*, which literally means "seed," such as one would sow in a garden.

Q 6.   When Yahweh Elohim pronounced the curse of Genesis 3:15, what did Adam and Eve understand Him to mean by **the woman**? With the illumination provided by the 12th chapter of Revelation, what did Yahweh Elohim mean by **the woman**?

Q 7.   What did Adam and Eve understand Yahweh Elohim to mean by the **seed of the woman**? With the illumination provided by passage in the 3rd chapter of Galatians and by the 12th chapter of Revelation, what did He mean by the **seed of the woman**?

Q 8.   What did Adam and Eve understand Yahweh Elohim to mean by **your seed** – that is, the seed or offspring of the serpent? With the illumination provided by the passages in the 13th chapter of Matthew, what did Yahweh Elohim mean by **your seed**?

Q 9.   Analyze the content of Genesis 3:15 with the further illumination provided by the passage in the 3rd chapter of Galatians, by the passages in the 13th chapter of Matthew, and by the 12th chapter of Revelation.

The Seed of the Woman

Because Genesis 3:15 is the seminal passage for both The Seed of the Woman motif and The Gospel motif, The Seed of the Woman motif is an important strand in the tapestry we are endeavoring to weave to reveal the glory of the Christian gospel. As became evident from the passages in the Christian Scriptures considered above, this motif is most profound, with multiple layers of meaning. Following are some of the important passages that contribute to the development of this motif:

Isaiah issues a prophetic announcement to Ahaz, king of Judah.

> **Isaiah 7:14**. Therefore Adonai Himself will give you a sign. Behold, the virgin shall conceive and bear a son, and shall call his name Immanuel. [Adapted from the ESV]

Isaiah's prophecy is quoted and interpreted by Matthew in his record of the angel's announcement to Joseph.

> **Matthew 1:23**. Behold, the virgin shall conceive and bear a son, and they shall call his name Immanuel (which means, God with us). [Adapted from the ESV]

The Apostle John succinctly represents the incarnation in the 1st chapter of his gospel.

> **John 1:1-4, 14**. In the beginning was the Logos, and the Logos was with God, and the Logos was God. He was in

the beginning with God. All things were made through Him, and without Him was not any thing made that was made. In Him was life, and the life was the light of men... And the Logos became flesh and dwelt among us, and we have seen His glory, glory as of the only Son from the Father, full of grace and truth. [Adapted from the ESV]

The fact that Messiah would destroy the works of the devil is set forth in the 2nd chapter of Hebrews.

Hebrew 2:14. Since therefore the children share in flesh and blood, He Himself likewise partook of the same things, that through death He might destroy the one who has the power of death, that is, the devil, and deliver all those who through fear of death were subject to lifelong slavery. [Adapted from the ESV]

The Apostle John prophesies the ultimate and complete defeat of Satan in the 20th chapter of Revelation.

Revelation 20:10. And the devil who had deceived them was thrown into the lake of fire and sulfur where the beast and the false prophet were, and they will be tormented day and night forever and ever. [ESV]

The Apostle Paul presents a summation of the trajectory of the Seed of the Woman motif in the 15th chapter of 1 Corinthians.

1 Corinthians 15:24-28. Then comes the end, when He delivers the kingdom to God the Father after destroying every rule and every authority and power. For He must reign until He has put all His enemies under His feet. The last enemy to be destroyed is death... When all things are subjected to Him, then the Son Himself will also be subjected to Him who put all things in subjection under Him, that God may be all in all. [Adapted from the ESV]

Allow your mind to reflect on the trajectory of The Seed of the Woman motif that is briefly summarized through the foregoing Scriptures. While Adam and Eve had a very limited and shortsighted understanding of Yahweh Elohim's pronouncement in Genesis 3:15, what He had in view was the ultimate defeat of Satan as recorded by the Apostle John in Revelation 20:10.

Notes & Reflections

Session 2. The Gospel Family of Motifs – Part Two

The Acceptable Sacrifice

Just a few short verses after the Protoevangelium in the 15th verse of the 3rd chapter of Genesis, we find this statement:

> **Genesis 3:21.** And Yahweh Elohim made for Adam and for his wife garments of skins and clothed them. [Adapted from the ESV]

Q 1.   What was involved in the process of Yahweh Elohim providing suitable garments for Adam and Eve? Discuss the emotional impact this would have had on Adam and Eve.

We need to turn back to the 2nd chapter of Genesis to find Yahweh Elohim's pronouncement regarding the forbidden fruit.

> **Genesis 2:15-17.** Yahweh Elohim took the man and put him in the garden of Eden to work it and keep it. And Yahweh Elohim commanded the man, saying, "You may surely eat of every tree of the garden, but of the tree of the knowledge of good and evil you shall not eat, for in the day that you eat of it you shall surely die." [Adapted from the ESV]

This passage underscores the severity of sin – it is a capital offense against Yahweh Elohim, deserving of nothing less than death! However, in His love, mercy, and grace, Yahweh Elohim withheld this deserved punishment of Adam's prideful rebellion against His clearly expressed commandment. Instead, He slaughtered one or more animals – the first physical death in creation – in order to provide suitable coverings for the first couple.

15

Genesis 3:21 is the seminal passage for The Acceptable Sacrifice motif. From the inception of this motif, Yahweh Elohim established the following three-part principle:

As was true of the first sin committed by mankind, all sin originates in a heart attitude of prideful rebellion against the righteous rule of Yahweh Elohim; therefore, it is a capital offense, for which the punishment is death.

Whereas Yahweh Elohim's absolute justice demands that a death take place when a person transgresses one of His commandments, His love, mercy, and grace motivates Him to pass over the offense.

Yahweh Elohim resolves this dilemma by providing that an innocent substitute die by the shedding of its blood in order to propitiate His absolute justice and allow Him to pardon the offense.

Whereas the attention of Adam and Eve was riveted upon the animals that Yahweh Elohim slaughtered before their very eyes, His attention was focused upon the bleeding form of His own dear Son as He died on a Roman cross many centuries later to atone for the sins of all mankind.

As we did with The Seed of the Woman motif, let us now turn to a succession of Scripture passages that trace the development and trajectory of The Acceptable Sacrifice motif.

The offerings of Cain and Abel, as recorded in the 4th chapter of Genesis.

> **Genesis 4:3-5.** In the course of time Cain brought to Yahweh an offering of the fruit of the ground, and Abel also brought of the firstborn of his flock and of their fat portions. And Yahweh had regard for Abel and his offering, but for Cain and his offering He had no regard.

16

So Cain was very angry, and his face fell. [Adapted from the ESV]

The experience of Cain and Abel underscores the importance of the third part of the principle of The Acceptable Sacrifice stated above, which is emphasized in the 9th chapter of Hebrews as follows:

Hebrews 9:22b. ...without the shedding of blood there is no forgiveness.

The Levitical offerings are documented in Leviticus 1-7. Here Yahweh gives very strict instructions on various offenses and their related sin offerings. Sin is costly! It cost the sinner a great deal in terms of his physical resources – a bull, a ram, a goat, etc. These were his livelihood. And yet Hebrews 10:4 informs us that "it is impossible for the blood of bulls and goats to take away sins."

Yahweh could allow His absolute justice to be propitiated by an animal sacrifice only because His eye was fixed upon the consummate sacrifice of His Son, of which the sacrificial animal served as a representation.

The sacrificial system was also personal. The one bringing the offering placed his head upon that of the animal while it was being slaughtered by the priest, thereby creating a powerful representation of Yahweh's transfer of the man's guilt to the animal.

The imagery of the Tabernacle in the wilderness, which we examined in Book 5, served as a representation of Jesus Christ and His sacrificial death in our stead. Consider the following eloquent statements in the Book of Hebrews:

> **Hebrews 7:23-25.** The former priests were many in number, because they were prevented by death from continuing in office, but He holds His priesthood permanently, because he continues forever. Consequently, He is able to save to the uttermost those who draw near to

God through Him, since He always lives to make intercession for them. [Adapted from the ESV]

Hebrews 9:28. ... So Christ, having been offered once to bear the sins of many, will appear a second time, not to deal with sin but to save those who are eagerly waiting for Him. [Adapted from the ESV]

The presentation of our bodies unto God as a living, holy, and acceptable sacrifice. In Romans 12:1-2 the Apostle Paul issues the following appeal to the Christ-followers in Rome:

Romans 12:1. Therefore I plead with you, brothers, in view of the aforementioned mercies of God, that you present your bodies unto God as a living, holy, and acceptable sacrifice – a service of worship rendered with the mind. And do not be conformed to this present age by allowing it to press your thinking process into its mold, but rather be transformed by the renewing of your mind, so that you may prove what is that good and acceptable and perfect will of God. [Adapted from The New Testament: An Expanded Translation by K. S. Wuest]

This passage in the 12th chapter of Romans is the terminus of The Acceptable Sacrifice motif. It began with Yahweh Elohim announcing the only way for fallen man to regain fellowship with Him, and it ends with us redeemed ones giving all that we are and have back to Him.

Q 2. In what ways does the living sacrifice called forth from us respond to Christ's sacrifice of Himself on our behalf? Is there any other fitting response to Christ's sacrifice?

Notes & Reflections

Session 3. The Gospel Family of Motifs – Part Three

Yahweh Elohim determined that He would confer the blessings of the Christian gospel through the seed of Abraham, who was the pioneer and progenitor of the People of the New Way. The first statement of Yahweh's covenant with Abraham is recorded in the 12th chapter of Genesis as follows:

> **Genesis 12:1-3**. Now Yahweh said to Abram, "Go from your country and your kindred and your father's house to the land that I will show you. And I will make of you a great nation, and I will bless you and make your name great, so that you will be a blessing. I will bless those who bless you, and him who dishonors you I will curse, and in you all the families of the earth shall be blessed."
> [Adapted from the ESV]

The Gospel Proclaimed to Abraham

Yahweh's promise to Abraham quoted above is the next clear statement of The Gospel motif after the Protoevangelium of Genesis 3:15.

Q 1.   Carefully study Genesis 12:1-3 and list the components of the gospel proclaimed to Abraham.

The Apostle Paul offers the following commentary on the gospel proclaimed to Abraham in the 3rd chapter of his letter to the Galatians:

> **Galatians 3:15-18**. To give a human example, brothers: even with a man-made covenant, no one annuls it or adds to it once it has been ratified. Now the promises were

19

made to Abraham and to his offspring. It does not say, "And to offsprings," referring to many, but referring to one, "And to your offspring," who is Christ. This is what I mean: the law, which came 430 years afterward, does not annul a covenant previously ratified by God, so as to make the promise void. For if the inheritance comes by the law, it no longer comes by promise; but God gave it to Abraham by a promise. [ESV]

Q 2.   The final component of the gospel proclaimed to Abraham is stated as follows: "In you all the families of the earth shall be blessed." According to Paul's commentary quoted above, through what means would this blessing of all peoples and nations be conferred?

The Gospel Proclaimed to Israel

In Session 4 of Book 3 we discussed the Kadesh-Barnea episode in considerable detail. In particular, we took note of the 15th chapter of Genesis, which records Yahweh's promise to Abraham to give the land of Canaan to his descendants – a promise secured by means of a solemn blood covenant. We also took note of Leviticus 26:3-8, which is one of the passages in the Torah that records Yahweh's promise to give the people of Israel military victory over their enemies, if only they were careful to keep His commandments and walk in His way – that is, if only they remained true to His covenant.

Then we considered the extended commentary on the Kadesh-Barnea episode recorded in Hebrews 3:7-4:13. In particular, Hebrews 4:2 represents the gospel proclaimed to Israel as parallel to that proclaimed to us.

Hebrews 4:2. For indeed we have had good news (= gospel) preached to us, just as they also; but the word they heard did not profit them, because it was not united by faith in those who heard. [NASB]

Q 3.   How would you represent the gospel preached to Israel?

The gospel preached to Israel was a two-part gospel as follows:

Deliverance out of bondage in Egypt.

Deliverance into rest in the promised land of Canaan after a period of conflict and conquest.

The parallel gospel preached to us also has two parts as follows:

Deliverance out of bondage to evil, sin, and death.

Deliverance into eternal rest in fellowship with God after a period of conflict and conquest.

And so, the gospel preached to Israel through Moses is, indeed, parallel to the gospel preached to us by Jesus Christ and His apostles.

Q 4.   To what extent have you experienced the two-part gospel described above in your own life?

Continuing our review of Book 3, Session 4, we discussed at length the effects of the Kadesh-Barnea episode and the failure of the

Israelites to lay hold of Yahweh's promise to deliver them into the land of promise. The ten spies who brought the bad report died immediately, and, except for Caleb and Joshua, that entire generation of Israelites were condemned to die off in the wilderness of Sinai.

Q 5.   What was the missing component in the ten spies' report?

For purposes of our present discussion of the gospel family of motifs, the significance of the Kadesh-Barnea episode is this: that generation of Israelites refused to believe that Yahweh could or would make good on His promise to deliver them into rest in the land of promise after a period of conflict and conquest. This would correspond to our refusing to believe that Yahweh can or will give us eternal rest after a period of conflict and conquest.

The Kadesh-Barnea generation of Israelites lacked the essential ingredient of the faith of their forefather, Abraham, which was his trust in Yahweh's ability to bring about resurrection from the dead.

Q 6.   Describe the role of faith in accepting the gospel message. Think back to our earlier studies. Whose faith is it?

Ephesians 2:8-9. For by grace you have been saved through faith. And this is not your own doing; it is the gift of God, not a result of works, so that no one may boast. [ESV]

There is nothing we can do to merit our salvation, or even contribute to it. It is truly the gift of God received through faith. Whose faith? As we discussed in Session 2 of Book 3, it is the faith of Jesus Christ imparted to us by means of the power-packed message about Christ in the hands of the Holy Spirit.

> **Romans 10:17.** So faith comes from what is heard, and what is heard comes through the message about Christ.

Notes & Reflections

Session 4. The Gospel Family of Motifs – Part Four

The Covenant of Conditional Blessing

A key passage in the development of The Covenant of Conditional Blessing motif is the passage quoted below from the 19th chapter of Exodus. This same passage is also the source or origin of the gospel of the kingdom of God. In other words, the gospel of the kingdom of God, which is an element of The Gospel motif, is intertwined with The Covenant of Conditional Blessing motif. Consider carefully Yahweh Elohim's remarkable announcement to the people of Israel in the following passage:

> **Exodus 19:3-6.** Yahweh called to Moses out of the mountain, saying, "Thus you shall say to the house of Jacob, and tell the people of Israel: You yourselves have seen what I did to the Egyptians, and how I bore you on eagles' wings and brought you to Myself. **Now therefore, if you will indeed obey My voice and keep My covenant, you shall be My treasured possession among all peoples, for all the earth is Mine; and you shall be to Me a kingdom of priests and a holy nation.** These are the words that you shall speak to the people of Israel." [Adapted from the ESV, emphasis added]

Q 1.   Upon what was the blessing of Yahweh Elohim on the nation of Israel dependent?

Obedience is not something that comes easily to most people due to our inherent prideful rebellion, which is at the very heart of our sin. This is a prime example of a conditional blessing, one which is hinged upon the tiny word "if." Again, choices matter!

Who had ever heard of God redeeming and delivering one nation of people out from another nation by means of great signs and wonders, and taking that nation unto Himself to be His treasured possession? Moses never got over this marvelous display of God's glorious grace. Notice the way in which he reflects upon it in the following passage in the 4th chapter of Deuteronomy:

> **Deuteronomy 4:5-8**. See, I have taught you statutes and rules, as Yahweh my Elohim commanded me, that you should do them in the land that you are entering to take possession of it. Keep them and do them, for that will be your wisdom and your understanding in the sight of the peoples, who, when they hear all these statutes, will say, "Surely this great nation is a wise and understanding people." For what great nation is there that has a god so near to it as the Yahweh our Elohim is to us, whenever we call upon Him? And what great nation is there, that has statutes and rules so righteous as all this law that I set before you today? [Adapted from the ESV]

The Law as Gospel

Because of the teaching of the Apostle Paul in regard to the law of Moses, it is difficult for us now to represent the law as gospel, but truly it was. The essential purpose of the Book of Genesis and the early chapters of Exodus is to set forth the background of the People of the New Way, the descendants of Abraham. As those descendants of Abraham, the people of Israel, gathered at the foot of Mt. Sinai, Yahweh Elohim announced that He was taking them unto Himself as His own treasured possession, and He was forming them, by means of the covenant of Mt. Sinai, into a kingdom of priests, through whom He would bless all peoples and nations.

Consider Paul's succinct statement of the purpose of the law in the 3rd chapter of Galatians as follows:

Galatians 3:24. The law, then, was our guardian until Christ, so that we could be justified by faith.

It is noteworthy that the Greek word translated "guardian" in this verse is *paidagogos*, from which we derive English words like "pedagogy." However, in the Greco-Roman culture of the 1st century AD this word designated a specific kind of household servant, whose task was to conduct the children of the household to and from school.

Q 2.   With this illumination, how would you represent the purpose of the law according to Paul?

A reading of Psalm 19:7-11 and the entirety of Psalm 119 is enough to convince us that, far from being regarded as a burden, the law was revered, treasured, valued, and loved. Consider, in particular, David's testimony concerning the preciousness of the torah or instruction of Yahweh:

> **Psalm 19:7-11**. The instruction of Yahweh is perfect, renewing one's life; the testimony of Yahweh is trustworthy, making the inexperienced wise. The precepts of Yahweh are right, making the heart glad; the command of Yahweh is radiant, making the eyes light up. The fear of Yahweh is pure, enduring forever; the ordinances of Yahweh are reliable and altogether righteous. They are more desirable than gold – even an abundance of pure gold; and sweeter they are than honey – even honey from the honeycomb. By them is Your servant warned; and in keeping them there is great reward. [Adapted from the HCSB]

Q 3.   In the passage from the 19th chapter of Exodus quoted above, Yahweh Elohim represents the nation of Israel as "a kingdom of priests and a holy nation." What is the significance of this representation?

Read 1 Peter 2:1-10 and Revelation 20:4.

Q 4.   The Apostle Peter employs similar language to that of Exodus 19:6 to represent us as Christ-followers. What is the significance of this representation?

Under the old covenant there were three leadership offices or functions ordained by Yahweh Elohim:

Prophet. The function of the prophet was to represent Yahweh Elohim to the people. In other words, his function was to speak to the people on behalf of Yahweh Elohim.

Priest. The function of the priest was to represent the people before Yahweh Elohim. In other words, the primary functions of the priest were to lead the people in worship of Yahweh Elohim and to offer intercession on behalf of the people before Yahweh's throne of grace.

King. The function of the king was to govern the nation in truth, righteousness, and justice in accordance with the law.

Q 5.   With this illumination of the priestly role, what is the significance of our serving as a kingdom of priests in accordance with 1 Peter 2:1-10.

Suzerain-Vassal Treaty

The covenant of Mt. Sinai, with its several components, is set forth according to the pattern or format of an ancient Hittite suzerain-vassal treaty; that is, a treaty between a king and his people. Such a treaty contained the stipulations of the covenant that the people were required to obey in order to receive the blessings of vassalry, of which protection against marauding enemies was paramount. After the stipulations, the covenant stated the blessings that the king would bestow if his people remained faithful to the terms of the covenant, together with the curses that would attend unfaithfulness.

In the context of our discussion of the gospel family of motifs, the point is this: according to the perspective of an ancient suzerain-vassal treaty, the law of Moses should, in fact, be represented as gospel.

Q 6.   Explain why the law of Moses should be represented as gospel. (**Hint**: Refer to King David's testimony in Psalm 19:7-11.)

The Covenant with David

The gospel of the kingdom of God is further shaped by the covenant that Yahweh cut with David as recorded in the following passage from the 7th chapter of 2 Samuel:

> **2 Samuel 7:8-16.** ... This is what Yahweh Sabaoth says: I took you from the pasture and from following the sheep to be ruler over My people Israel... When your days are fulfilled and you lie down with your fathers, I will raise up your offspring after you, who shall come from your body, and I will establish his kingdom. He shall build a house for My name, and I will establish the throne of his

kingdom forever. I will be to him a father, and he shall be to Me a son... But My steadfast love will not depart from him... And your house and your kingdom shall be made sure forever before Me. Your throne shall be established forever. [Adapted from the ESV]

The 2nd Psalm, that great Messianic psalm, serves as a poetic commentary on the Davidic Covenant. Note in both the passage quoted above and in the 2nd Psalm how David's son, Solomon, serves as a near-term prefigurement of a greater Son of David who would arise in the future. He would sit upon David's throne in Jerusalem; but His rule would embrace all nations, and His dominion would extend to the ends of the earth.

Prophetic Shaping of the Gospel of the Kingdom of God

As we trace the trajectory of the gospel of the kingdom of God through the prophetic literature of the Hebrew Scriptures, it is further shaped and articulated. An important feature of this prophetic shaping and articulation is the **theology of restoration**. Although Israel was unfaithful to the terms of the covenant with Yahweh, and therefore would be made to suffer the terrible consequences specified in the suzerain-vassal treaty, Yahweh would not forsake her utterly, but rather He would bring about a future restoration. This theme is beautifully and poignantly set forth in the following passage from Isaiah 54:7-8.

> **Isaiah 54:7-8**. "For a brief moment I deserted you, but with great compassion I will gather you. In overflowing anger for a moment I hid my face from you, but with everlasting love I will have compassion on you," says Yahweh, your Redeemer. [Adapted from the ESV]

A sublime representation of the glorious future Messianic Kingdom is presented by Micah.

> **Micah 4:1-4**. It shall come to pass in the latter days that the mountain of the house of Yahweh shall be established

30

as the highest of the mountains, and it shall be lifted up above the hills; and peoples shall flow to it, and many nations shall come, and say: "Come, let us go up to the mountain of Yahweh, to the house of the Elohim of Jacob, that He may teach us His ways and that we may walk in His paths." For out of Zion shall go forth the law, and the word of Yahweh from Jerusalem. He shall judge between many peoples and shall decide for strong nations far away; and they shall beat their swords into plowshares, and their spears into pruning hooks; nation shall not lift up sword against nation, neither shall they learn war anymore; but they shall sit every man under his vine and under his fig tree, and no one shall make them afraid, for the mouth of Yahweh Sabaoth has spoken.   [Adapted from the ESV]

The historical restoration of Israel recorded in the books of Ezra and Nehemiah serves as prefigurement of the glorious Messianic Kingdom that is set forth in the 20th chapter of Revelation.

> **Revelation 20:4.** Then I saw thrones, and seated on them were those to whom the authority to judge was committed. Also I saw the souls of those who had been beheaded for the testimony of Jesus and for the word of God, and those who had not worshiped the beast or its image and had not received its mark on their foreheads or their hands. They came to life and reigned with Christ for a thousand years. [ESV]

We have traced a number of important strands of teaching that correspond to the gospel family of motifs through the entire Bible. By this means, we have glimpsed the glory of the Christian gospel, including its ancient roots in the *Protoevangelium* of Genesis 3:15 and the Sinaitic Covenant expressed in Exodus 19:3-6. However, this discussion has been far from exhaustive. Instead, we have barely scratched the surface of the development of the gospel family of motifs, leaving ample space for you, the student, to add your own insights as they may arise over the course of your devotional study of Scripture.

However, even this brief sketch has placed in evidence that the scope of the Christian gospel is both cosmic and eternal. One day God will do away with the present heavens and earth, corrupted as they are by evil, sin, and death. And He will create new heavens and earth wherein righteousness dwells. These will be populated by a redeemed worshiping community called forth and made up of people from all nations and ethnic groups. This multitude will enjoy fellowship with God and delight in His glorious grace forever and forever. He will dwell with them and be their God, and they will be His people. The effects of the Fall will be totally obliterated, and the curse pronounced by Yahweh Elohim in Genesis 3:14ff will be utterly reversed and neutralized. This is the ultimate focus and goal of the Christian gospel.

Notes & Reflections

Session 5. The Two-Part Christian Gospel – Part One

In the previous four sessions we have examined the gospel family of integrative motifs as a means to portray the glory of the Christian gospel, including its ancient roots and its many facets. The message about Jesus Christ is the gospel, beautiful and multifaceted like a precious diamond, and deserving of our lifelong devotion to understand it, share it, and practice it.

With this background, we are now ready to discuss the two aspects of the Christian gospel: namely, the gospel of the kingdom of God and the gospel of God. These two aspects are summarized in Table 1.

Table 1. Summary of the two Aspects of the Christian Gospel

Parameter	Gospel of the Kingdom of God	Gospel of God
Roots	Rooted in the suzerain/vassal treaty enacted by Yahweh with Israel at Mt. Sinai.	Rooted in the *protoevangelium* of Genesis 3:15, and in Yahweh's blood covenant with Abraham recorded in Genesis 15.
Emphasis	The truth, righteousness, and justice of God in His rule over men and nations.	The sovereign grace of God in obliterating the effects of evil, sin, and death, and granting eternal life to those who trust, love, and fear Him.
Scope	Cosmic and eternal, spanning all time and space.	

Parameter	Gospel of the Kingdom of God	Gospel of God
Confronts	Prideful rebellion against the righteous rule of God—the core of human iniquity.	Human bondage to evil, sin, and death.
Focus	Jesus Christ as King of kings and Lord of lords as presented in the Synoptic Gospels (Matthew, Mark and Luke) and the Book of Acts.	The atoning death, burial, and resurrection of Jesus Christ, which makes possible God's gracious gifts of righteousness, regeneration, sanctification, and glorification.
Response	**Repent and believe** (Mark 1:14-15) by turning from prideful rebellion with wholehearted repentance and submitting to Christ's kingly rule.	**Confess, receive, and believe** (John 1:10-13 & Romans 10:9) by wholeheartedly embracing Jesus Christ as both Savior and Lord.
Perversion	Legalism (too much law)	Antinomianism (no law)

The remainder of this session and the three which follow it will unfold as follows:

First, in the remainder of this session we discuss Scripture passages that relate to the Christian gospel as a whole.

Second, in Session 6 we discuss Scripture passages that relate specifically to the gospel of the kingdom of God.

Third, in Session 7 we discuss Scripture passages that relate specifically to the gospel of God.

Fourth, in Session 8 we discuss the two cardinal perversions of the Christian gospel.

As we examine a succession of Scripture passages in accordance with the above outline, there is a set of four questions that we will bring to bear on each passage:

First, why is the passage good news?

Second, are there any promised blessings in the passage? If so, what are they and why are they beneficial?

Third, are there any conditions attached to receiving the blessings? If so, what are they?

Fourth, to what degree does the passage require obedience to God's commands?

The Eternal Gospel

The heading for this section, in which we discuss the Christian gospel as a whole, is inspired by the following passage from the 14th chapter of Revelation:

> **Revelation 14:6-7.** Then I saw another angel flying directly overhead, with an eternal **gospel** to proclaim to those who dwell on earth, to every nation and tribe and language and people. And he said with a loud voice, "Fear God and give Him glory, because the hour of His judgment has come, and **worship** Him who made heaven and earth, the sea and the springs of water." [Adapted from the ESV, emphasis added]

The gospel was in the heart of God in eternity past, it was alluded to throughout the Hebrew scriptures, and it was actualized in the incarnate Son of God's sinless life, death, burial, and resurrection that made atonement for the sin of all mankind. It will be consummated in the future with the coming of a new heaven and earth wherein all the effects of evil, sin and death are completely obliterated, and God reigns supreme in perfect righteousness and justice.

That said, let us now practice answer the four questions listed above with regard to Revelation 14:6-7:

Q 1.   What about this passage is good news?

Q 2.   Are there any promised blessings in the passage? If so, what are they and why are they beneficial?

Q 3.   Are there any conditions attached to receiving the blessings? If so, what are they and what are their implications?

Q 4.   To what degree does the passage require obedience to God's commands?

The gospel is timeless and universal in scope, and it is freely offered to every nation, tribe, language, and people group. Although its blessings are not explicitly stated in our focal passage, they are implicit in the eternal gospel's being offered as a means to escape the severe plagues that are described in the later chapters of the book of Revelation. In this passage, God requires three responses to the eternal gospel: to fear Him, give Him glory, and worship Him. Although the passage does not directly address living an obedient lifestyle, such is implied by the command to fear, glorify, and worship God.

It is impossible to fear, glorify, and worship God without also submitting to His righteous rule, loving Him, keeping His commands, and walking in His way.

Read Romans 8:19-21, Colossians 1:20, Titus 2:11-14, Titus 3:4-7, Hebrews 6:17-20, and Hebrews 7:24-25.

Q 5.   Do you agree that each of these passages seems to apply to the Christian gospel as a whole rather than specifically to either the gospel of the kingdom of God or the gospel of God? Explain your answer.

Q 6.   Now use the space below to bring each of the four questions to bear upon each passage.

The Christian gospel transcends time and space, and it is universal in scope. By embracing it, man is restored to a right relationship with God and his fellow man, and he is brought into harmony with the created order as God originally intended. The Christian gospel was settled in the councils of eternity past as the plan by which God would conclusively conquer the mystery of iniquity, obliterate evil, sin and death, and bring into being a new heaven and earth where righteousness and truth would dwell. It is immutable or unchanging because it is bound up in the person of Jesus Christ, who is the same yesterday, today, and forever (Hebrews 13:8).

Our Need for the Gospel

Before moving on from consideration of the Christian gospel as a whole, we should give some thought to this question: Why do we need the gospel?

The argument of the Apostle Paul in the opening chapters of Romans from Romans 1:18 to Romans 3:20 is entirely devoted to answering this question. Consider the following verses:

> **Romans 1:18**. For the wrath of God is revealed from heaven against all ungodliness and unrighteousness of men, who by their unrighteousness suppress the truth. [ESV]

Romans 1:32. Though they know God's righteous decree that those who practice such things deserve to die, they not only do them but give approval to those who practice them. [ESV]

Romans 2:1. Therefore you have no excuse, O man, every one of you who judges. For in passing judgment on another you condemn yourself, because you, the judge, practice the very same things. [ESV]

Romans 3:9-10. What then? Are we Jews any better off? No, not at all. For we have already charged that all, both Jews and Greeks, are under sin, as it is written: "None is righteous, no, not one..." [ESV]

Romans 3:19-20. Now we know that whatever the law says it speaks to those who are under the law, so that every mouth may be stopped, and the whole world may be held accountable to God. For by works of the law no human being will be justified in His sight, since through the law comes knowledge of sin. [Adapted from ESV]

Romans 3:23. For all have sinned and fall short of the glory of God.

Q 7.   Summarize the trajectory of Paul's argument based upon these passages.

Concluding Remarks Regarding the Eternal Gospel

Before turning to the gospel of the kingdom of God in the next session, a fitting conclusion to this session is the following statement concerning the Christian gospel from the pen of John R. Stott:

... The Bible does not just contain the gospel; it is the gospel. Through the Bible God is Himself actually evangelizing, that is, communicating the good news to the world. You will recall Paul's statement about Genesis 12:3 that "the Scripture preached the gospel beforehand to Abraham" (Galatians 3:8, RSV). All Scripture preaches the gospel; God evangelizes through it. [From Perspectives on the World Christian Movement, Third Edition, page 23]

Notes & Reflections

Session 6. The Two-Part Christian Gospel – Part Two

In this session we will discuss the **gospel of the kingdom of God**, which is the aspect of the Christian gospel that is emphasized in the Synoptic Gospels (Matthew, Mark, and Luke) and the Book of Acts. Because the gospel of the kingdom of God is rooted in the covenant that Yahweh Elohim enacted with the people of Israel through Moses at Mt. Sinai, it is the form of the gospel that appeals most powerfully to the Jewish mind. Accordingly, Matthew's gospel presents Jesus Christ as the son of David, and therefore qualified to sit on the throne of David in fulfillment of the Messianic kingdom prophecies in the Hebrew Scriptures. Moreover, Matthew presents Jesus Christ as a lawgiver like Moses, and therefore the One who fulfills the promise of Yahweh Elohim in Deuteronomy 18:15-19.

The other aspect of the Christian gospel that is introduced in the Gospel of John and is developed in the Pauline Epistles is the **gospel of God**, which we will discuss in Session 7. Table 1 summarizes both aspects of the Christian gospel to place in evidence how they complement one another and is repeated below for your convenience.

Table 1. Summary of the Two Aspects of the Christian Gospel

Parameter	Gospel of the Kingdom of God	Gospel of God
Roots	Rooted in the suzerain/vassal treaty enacted by Yahweh with Israel at Mt. Sinai.	Rooted in the *protoevangelium* of Genesis 3:15, and in Yahweh's blood covenant with Abraham recorded in Genesis 15.

Parameter	Gospel of the Kingdom of God	Gospel of God
Emphasis	The truth, righteousness, and justice of God in His rule over men and nations.	The sovereign grace of God in obliterating the effects of evil, sin, and death, and granting eternal life to those who trust, love, and fear Him.
Scope	Cosmic and eternal, spanning all time and space.	
Confronts	Prideful rebellion against the righteous rule of God—the core of human iniquity.	Human bondage to evil, sin, and death.
Focus	Jesus Christ as King of kings and Lord of lords as presented in the Synoptic Gospels (Matthew, Mark and Luke) and the Book of Acts.	The atoning death, burial, and resurrection of Jesus Christ, which makes possible God's gracious gifts of righteousness, regeneration, sanctification, and glorification.
Response	**Repent and believe** (Mark 1:14-15) by turning from prideful rebellion with wholehearted repentance and submitting to Christ's kingly rule.	**Confess, receive, and believe** (John 1:10-13 & Romans 10:9) by wholeheartedly embracing Jesus Christ as both Savior and Lord.
Perversion	Legalism (too much law)	Antinomianism (no law)

The Gospel of the Kingdom of God

As summarized in the table above, the gospel of the kingdom of God confronts man's prideful rebellion against the righteous rule of God. It focuses upon Jesus Christ as King of kings and Lord of lords. Our proper response to it involves our submitting to Christ's kingly authority in all spheres of life and ministry. To initiate our discussion of the gospel of the kingdom of God, consider the following Scripture passages:

Matthew 4:12-17. When He heard that John had been arrested, He withdrew into Galilee. He left Nazareth behind and went to live in Capernaum by the sea, in the region of Zebulun and Naphtali. This was to fulfill what was spoken through the prophet Isaiah: Land of Zebulun and land of Naphtali, along the sea road, beyond the Jordan, Galilee of the Gentiles! The people who live in darkness have seen a great light, and for those living in the shadowland of death, light has dawned. From then on Jesus began to preach, "Repent, because the kingdom of heaven has come near!"

Matthew 6:9-10. Therefore, you should pray like this: Our Father in heaven, Your name be honored as holy. Your kingdom come. Your will be done on earth as it is in heaven.

Matthew 7:21-27. Not everyone who says to Me, "Lord, Lord!" will enter the kingdom of heaven, but only the one who does the will of My Father in heaven. On that day many will say to Me, "Lord, Lord, didn't we prophesy in Your name, drive out demons in Your name, and do many miracles in Your name?" Then I will announce to them, "I never knew you! Depart from Me, you lawbreakers! Therefore, everyone who hears these words of Mine and acts on them will be like a sensible man who built his house on the rock. The rain fell, the rivers rose, and the winds blew and pounded that house. Yet it didn't collapse, because its foundation was on the rock. But everyone who hears these words of Mine and doesn't act on them will be like a foolish man who built his house on the sand. The rain fell, the rivers rose, the winds blew and pounded that house, and it collapsed. And its collapse was great!

Matthew 24:14. This good news of the kingdom will be proclaimed in all the world as a testimony to all nations. And then the end will come.

Mark 1:14-15. After John was arrested, Jesus went to Galilee, preaching the good news of God: "The time is fulfilled, and the kingdom of God has come near. Repent and believe in the good news!"

Luke 16:16-17. The Law and the Prophets were until John; since then, the good news of the kingdom of God has been proclaimed, and everyone is strongly urged to enter it. But it is easier for heaven and earth to pass away than for one stroke of a letter in the law to drop out.

Acts 1:3-8. After He had suffered, He also presented Himself alive to them by many convincing proofs, appearing to them during 40 days and speaking about the kingdom of God. While He was together with them, He commanded them not to leave Jerusalem, but to wait for the Father's promise. "This," He said, 'is what you heard from Me; for John baptized with water, but you will be baptized with the Holy Spirit not many days from now." So when they had come together, they asked Him, "Lord, are You restoring the kingdom to Israel at this time?" He said to them, "It is not for you to know times or periods that the Father has set by His own authority. But you will receive power when the Holy Spirit has come on you, and you will be My witnesses in Jerusalem, in all Judea and Samaria, and to the ends of the earth."

Acts 28:30-31. Then he stayed two whole years in his own rented house. And he welcomed all who visited him, proclaiming the kingdom of God and teaching the things concerning the Lord Jesus Christ with full boldness and without hindrance.

All of these passages are drawn from the Synoptic Gospels and Acts, and each of them mentions the kingdom of God or the kingdom of heaven.

Q 1.   Having examined all of these Scripture passages, list your observations below.

The benefit of unspeakable value that is offered to all people through the gospel of the kingdom of God is the privilege of actually entering and becoming a citizen of that kingdom.

Q 2.   For a person who repents of his prideful rebellion against the righteous rule of God and submits his life completely to Jesus Christ as King, is the benefit of entering and becoming a citizen of the kingdom of God fully actualized immediately? Explain your answer.

Q 3.   Are there conditions attached to kingdom citizenship? If so, what are they?

Covenant of Conditional Blessing

This is the last of the integrative motifs which are listed near the beginning of Session 1. We touched on this particular motif in

45

Session 4 and noted its connection to the suzerain / vassal treaty that Yahweh Elohim enacted with the people of Israel at Mt. Sinai. To review, there are three essential components of such a treaty:

First, it stipulates the commandments that the people are to obey in order to receive the benefits of the treaty, most important of which is the king's protection from external threats.

Second, it includes an enumeration of the blessings the king promises to bestow so long as the people abide by the terms of the treaty.

Third, it includes an enumeration of the curses the king will inflict should the people rebel against the terms of the treaty.

Concerning the suzerain / vassal treaty between Yahweh Elohim and the people of Israel, the most expansive statement of the blessings and curses is found in the 28th through 30th chapters of Deuteronomy – a speech that Moses delivered to the people of Israel while they were encamped on the plains of Moab on the east side of the Jordan River opposite the city of Jericho. This speech was designed to prepare the people of Israel for success in their upcoming battles with the Canaanites.

Peruse the 28th through 30th chapters of Deuteronomy.

Q 4.   Do you note any parallels between Moses' instruction and exhortation to the people of Israel in this extended passage and Jesus' instruction in Matthew 7:21-27? If so, what are they?

Table 2 places in evidence the parallels between the old and new covenants in regard to the content of the gospel and the conditions for kingdom citizenship.

Table 2. Covenant of Conditional Blessing

Old Covenant	New Covenant
Gospel: ■ Deliverance from bondage in Egypt. ■ Deliverance into rest in the promised land after a period of conflict and conquest	**Gospel:** ■ Deliverance from bondage to evil, sin, and death. ■ Deliverance into eternal rest after a period of conflict and conquest.
Conditions for kingdom citizenship: ■ Deuteronomy 28-30.	**Conditions for kingdom citizenship:** ■ Matthew 5-7.

Moses stands as keeper of the gate into the promised land, and his speech at the end of Deuteronomy defines the conditions for kingdom citizenship – that is, actually enjoying the rest promised in the second part of the old covenant gospel. In like manner, Jesus Christ stands as keeper of the gate into God's eternal kingdom, and His Sermon on the Mount defines the conditions for kingdom citizenship – that is, actually enjoying the rest promised in the second part of the new covenant gospel. I need to hasten to add that even as the rest of the Hebrew Scriptures enlarges upon and develops the conditions for kingdom citizenship announced by Moses, in like manner the rest of the Christian Scriptures enlarges upon and develops the conditions for kingdom citizenship announced by Jesus in His teachings.

There is essential continuity from the old covenant to the new in regard to the covenant of conditional blessing. It is not enough to give mental assent to the gospel. We must obey it as well.

Repent and Believe

> **Mark 1:14-15.** After John was arrested, Jesus went to Galilee, preaching the good news of God: "The time is fulfilled, and the kingdom of God has come near. Repent and believe in the good news!"

Q 5.   What was the content of the "good news of God" which Jesus preached?

Q 6.   What is the meaning of His statement, "The kingdom of God has come near?"

Q 7.   What is the meaning of His exhortation, "Repent and believe in the good news?"

Q 8.   What did "repent and believe" mean to you when you first heard the gospel, and what does it mean to you today?

The Greek word that is translated "repent" in the Christian Scriptures is *metanoeo*; it designates a complete change of mind. In our former state of prideful rebellion and unbelief, we represented our sinful state before God as natural, even normal. However, after having been impacted by the power-packed message about Christ (Romans 10:17), our representation radically changed. Our state of prideful rebellion and sin became hideous and intolerable. Whereas in our prideful rebellion against the rule of God, we were content to live as if He didn't exist, now our heart longs for Him as the deer pants for streams of water (Psalm 42:1ff).

The following passage from the 2nd chapter of Acts places in evidence the true nature of repentance:

> **Acts 2:37-39.** Now when they heard this they were cut to the heart, and said to Peter and the rest of the apostles, "Brothers, what shall we do?" And Peter said to them, "**Repent** and be baptized every one of you in the name of Jesus Christ for the forgiveness of your sins, and you will receive the gift of the Holy Spirit. For the promise is for you and for your children and for all who are far off, everyone whom the Lord our God calls to Himself." [Adapted from the RSV, emphasis added]

Q 9.   Analyze the Apostle Peter's statement that is quoted in this passage. Why did he answer in this way, and what is the meaning of his answer?

Yahweh Elohim has established His kingdom on earth, beginning with the suzerain / vassal treaty He enacted with the people of Israel at Mt. Sinai. He promised to bless, provide for, and protect them in exchange for their absolute love, allegiance, and obedience. We know that Israel made many unfortunate choices in preferring to go their own way or the way of the surrounding nations rather than walking in the way of Yahweh. The results were disastrous. Yet Yahweh Elohim neither abandoned His people nor His plan for His kingdom on earth. Through the sacrificial death, burial, and resurrection of His Son, Jesus Christ, He has made His kingdom accessible to anyone who would repent of his prideful rebellion, believe the gospel, and receive the forgiveness of sin. The suzerain / vassal treaty is still in effect wherein Jesus is King, and His followers are the vassals. Christ bestows the blessings of kingdom citizenship as a function of our obedience to the gospel.

This aspect of the gospel is one that is often disregarded in our Christian churches. A perfect king demands wholehearted allegiance and obedience from His subjects. It is not only our duty to serve Him, but it is our privilege and joy.

Notes & Reflections

Session 7. The Two-Part Christian Gospel – Part Three

Table 1 summarizes the complementary features of the two aspects of the Christian gospel, and is repeated below for your convenience:

Summary of the Two Aspects of the Christian Gospel

Parameter	Gospel of the Kingdom of God	Gospel of God
Roots	Rooted in the suzerain/vassal treaty enacted by Yahweh with Israel at Mt. Sinai.	Rooted in the *protoevangelium* of Genesis 3:15, and in Yahweh's blood covenant with Abraham recorded in Genesis 15.
Emphasis	The truth, righteousness, and justice of God in His rule over men and nations.	The sovereign grace of God in obliterating the effects of evil, sin, and death, and granting eternal life to those who trust, love, and fear Him.
Scope	Cosmic and eternal, spanning all time and space.	
Confronts	Prideful rebellion against the righteous rule of God—the core of human iniquity.	Human bondage to evil, sin, and death.

Parameter	Gospel of the Kingdom of God	Gospel of God
Focus	Jesus Christ as King of kings and Lord of lords as presented in the Synoptic Gospels (Matthew, Mark and Luke) and the Book of Acts.	The atoning death, burial, and resurrection of Jesus Christ, which makes possible God's gracious gifts of righteousness, regeneration, sanctification, and glorification.
Response	**Repent and believe** (Mark 1:14-15) by turning from prideful rebellion with wholehearted repentance and submitting to Christ's kingly rule.	**Confess, receive, and believe** (John 1:10-13 & Romans 10:9) by wholeheartedly embracing Jesus Christ as both Savior and Lord.
Perversion	Legalism (too much law)	Antinomianism (no law)

The Gospel of God

The **gospel of God** is introduced in the Gospel of John, and it is discussed and developed in the Pauline Epistles. Whereas the gospel of the kingdom of God appeals most strongly to the Jewish mind, the gospel of God appeals most strongly to the Gentile mind.

This aspect of the Christian gospel has been emphasized in evangelistic preaching since the time of Charles Finney in the first half of the 19th century, and so it is the aspect of the gospel with which we are most familiar. The following two verses from the 3rd chapter of John and the 10th chapter of Romans could be regarded as keynote verses in the proclamation of the gospel of God:

John 3:16. For God loved the world in this way: He gave His One and Only Son, so that everyone who believes into Him will not perish but have eternal life. [Adapted from the HCSB]

Romans 10:13. For everyone who calls on the name of Yahweh will be saved. [Adapted from the HCSB]

As we will discuss in Session 8, the proclamation of the Christian gospel has emphasized deliverance from evil, sin, and death through Jesus' sacrifice of Himself, but it has generally failed to emphasize the need for our submission to Jesus' authority as King and our obedience to His commands.

Trajectory of the Gospel of God

As summarized in the table above, and as we discussed in Session 1, the gospel of God is rooted in the Protoevangelium of Genesis 3:15, which looks forward to the woman's seed, Jesus Christ, and His victory over the serpent, Satan.

Genesis 3:15, "I will put enmity between you and the woman, and between your offspring and her offspring; He shall bruise your head, and you shall bruise His heel." [Adapted from the ESV]

With this Scripture serving as the inception of the gospel of God, clearly its terminus must be in the final destruction of Satan and his minions in the lake of fire as recorded in the final chapters of the book of Revelation.

In what follows, I either quote or refer to a number of Scripture passages in canonical order which trace the trajectory of the gospel of God. This list is by no means exhaustive, and you should endeavor to add other Scripture passages from your own studies. As you examine each passage, reflect on the following question:

How does this Scripture passage contribute to the development of the gospel of God?

53

At the conclusion of this session, you will be asked to write a brief essay that expresses you answer to this question for the entire collection of Scripture passages. You will be asked to answer other questions that are specifically keyed to particular Scripture passages.

Our second Scripture passage along the gospel of God trajectory is one of the most important in the entire Bible.

> **Genesis 15:6**. And he (Abraham) believed Yahweh, and He (Yahweh) counted it to him as righteousness.
> [Adapted from the ESV]

Q 1.   What was the content of the gospel proclaimed by Yahweh Himself to Abram?

Q 2.   In the light of the Apostle Paul's commentary on Genesis 15:6 in Romans 4:1-24, what was the content of Abraham's faith response?

Read Isaiah 53:1-12; Jeremiah 31:31-34; and Ezekiel 11:19-21 & 36:26-28.

> **John 1:10-13**. He was in the world, and the world was created through Him, yet the world did not recognize Him. He came to His own, and His own people did not receive Him, But to all who did receive Him, He gave them the right to be children of God, to those who believe in His name, who were born, not of blood, or of the will of the flesh, or of the will of man, but of God.

Read John 3:14-21, Acts 10:43 & 16:29-34, and Romans 3:21-26 & 4:1-24.

Q 3. Referring to John 3:16, the Greek preposition in the phrase translated "believe in Him" is actually *eis*, which means "into." In the light of this, what meaning did the Apostle John intend to convey in John 3:16 regarding our faith response to the gospel?

Q 4. Referring to Acts 16:30, the response of Paul and Silas to the Philippian jailor's question as rendered correctly in the HCSB was that he should "believe on the Lord Jesus." What meaning did Doctor Luke intend to convey by this statement regarding our faith response to the gospel?

Q 5. Given the context of Acts 16:29-34, what did the jailor mean by his question, "What must I do to be saved?" What did Paul and Silas mean by their answer to the jailor's question?

Q 6.   List the transformative results of Paul's and Silas' gospel proclamation in the life of the Philippian jailor.

Romans 8:3-4. What the law could not do since it was limited by the flesh, God did. He condemned sin in the flesh by sending His own Son in flesh like ours under sin's domain, and as a sin offering, in order that the law's requirement would be accomplished in us who do not walk according to the flesh but according to the Spirit.

Romans 10:9. If you confess with your mouth "Jesus is Lord," and believe in your heart that God raised Him from the dead, you will be saved.

Q 7.   What three key verbs in John 1:10-13 and Romans 10:9 represent the only appropriate response to the gospel of God?

Romans 10:17. So faith comes from what is heard, and what is heard comes through the message about Christ.

1 Cor. 15:22 For as in Adam all die, so also in Christ shall all be made alive. [ESV]

2 Corinthians 5:14-15. For Christ's love constrains and compels us, since we have reached this conclusion: If One died for all, then all died. And He died for all so that those who live should no longer live for themselves, but for the One who died for them and was raised. [Adapted from the HCSB]

Galatians 2:16-20. ... We have believed into Christ Jesus so that we might be justified by the faith of Christ and not by the works of the law, because by the works of the law no human being will be justified. ... For through the law I have died to the law, so that I might live for God. I have been crucified with Christ and I no longer live, but Christ lives in me. So then, the life I now live in the body, I live by the faith of the Son of God, who loved me and gave Himself for me. [Adapted from the HCSB]

Read Ephesians 1:3-6 & 2:1-7.

Ephesians 2:8-10. For by grace you have been saved through faith. And this is not your own doing; it is the gift of God, not a result of works, so that no one may boast. For we are His workmanship, created in Christ Jesus for good works, *which God prepared beforehand, that we should walk in them*. [Adapted from the ESV]

Q 8.   The words belief, faith, and trust are synonyms that describe the appropriate human response to the gospel of God. In the light of your studies thus far, what connotations do these words bring to your mind?

Q 9.   Recall our discussion of the two kinds of faith in Session 2 of Book 3. Whose faith is imparted to and energized within us and where does it come from in the light of Romans 10:17?

Q 10.   In the light of Romans 3:21-26 and Ephesians 2:8-10, what is included in the grace of God?

Q 11.   What is the origin of the good works spoken of in Ephesians 2:10?

Read Colossians 1:15-20, Titus 2:11-14 & 3:4-6, 1 Peter 1:3-12, Hebrews 2:14-15 & 7:20-25, and Revelation 20:1-3, 20:7-10, & 21:1-8.

Q 12.   Write a brief essay summarizing the way in which the Scripture passages quoted and listed above contribute to the unfolding of the scope and richness of the gospel of God.

Concluding Comments Regarding the Gospel of God

From the Scripture passages we have examined in this session, we have discovered the scope and richness of gospel of God. It encompasses all time and all space, it is the product of the grace of God from start to finish, and it brings about the complete and absolute eradication of all the effects of evil, sin, and death, not only in the lives of human beings, but throughout the entire cosmos as well.

The gospel of God offers deliverance from bondage to evil, sin and death and deliverance into eternal rest after a period of conflict and conquest in this present life.

Notes & Reflections

Session 8. Perversions of the Christian Gospel

During the 1st century AD while the Apostle Paul was writing his epistles, the two perversions of the gospel which he and the other apostles had to confront were antinomianism and legalism.

Antinomianism

The theological term "antinomianism" is the Greek word for law, which is *nomos*. Accordingly, the term literally means "against law." It is the belief that under the gospel of grace, moral law is not at all binding on Christians because faith alone is sufficient for salvation. This view holds that our liberty in Christ makes obedience to Christ's commands completely optional. One only needs to trust in the gospel for salvation, which is entirely by God's grace. Saving faith is hereby reduced to mere mental assent to the facts of the gospel.

The Apostle Paul addresses antinomianism in the following passage in the 6th chapter of Romans:

> **Romans 6:1.** What should we say then? Should we continue in sin so that grace may abound? Absolutely not! How can we who died to sin still live in it? [Adapted from the HCSB]

Q 1.   Paraphrase the argument that Paul brings to bear upon antinomianism in this passage. From our study of the trajectory of the gospel of God in the previous session, what other arguments counter the antinomian position?

Q 2.   Describe some examples of antinomianism from your own experience and culture.

Q 3.   In what ways does antinomianism impact the proclamation of the gospel and the faith response of people to the gospel?

Legalism

"Legalism" is a theological term that literally means "too much law." During the ministry of the Apostle Paul, legalism was embodied in the teaching of the Judaizers, who insisted that Gentile disciples had to keep the law of Moses, and that their male babies had to be circumcised. In other words, law-keeping was imposed as an additional requirement for salvation, over and above justification by grace through faith. Paul confronts the heresy of the Judaizers in his letter to the Galatians, and he presents the theological basis for the Christian's relationship to the law in the 7th and 8th chapters of Romans.

In our day and time, legalism can take either of two forms:

Legalistic requirements imposed on **salvation**; in other words, we are justified by some combination of God's grace and human works.

Legalistic requirements or rules imposed on **sanctification**; in other words, godly Christians don't engage in certain behaviors and do engage in certain other behaviors.

Q 4.   List the forms of legalism that you observe in your culture or community.

Q 5.   Reflecting on the teachings of Jesus – especially His rebukes of the Pharisees – what state of mind and heart is likely to attend the practice of legalism?

Q 6.   Drawing from the Scripture passages that we surveyed in the previous session in developing the trajectory of the gospel of God, assemble an argument against legalism.

Q 7.   In what ways does legalism impact the proclamation of the gospel and the faith response of people to the gospel?

Concluding Remarks Regarding Antinomianism and Legalism

Both antinomianism and legalism are perversions of the gospel which surfaced in the 1st century and which continue in various forms even to our day and time. Moreover, both of these perversions are based on a misunderstanding of the proper relationship of the Christ follower to the moral law – a subject we discussed in Session 6 of Book 3. And each of them results from a failure to embrace both the gospel of the kingdom of God and the gospel of God.

Table 1 first appeared in Session 5 and compares the two aspects of the Christian gospel.

Summary of the Two Aspects of the Christian Gospel

Parameter	Gospel of the Kingdom of God	Gospel of God
Roots	Rooted in the suzerain/vassal treaty enacted by Yahweh with Israel at Mt. Sinai.	Rooted in the *protoevangelium* of Genesis 3:15, and in Yahweh's blood covenant with Abraham recorded in Genesis 15.
Emphasis	The truth, righteousness, and justice of God in His rule over men and nations.	The sovereign grace of God in obliterating the effects of evil, sin, and death, and granting eternal life to those who trust, love, and fear Him.
Scope	Cosmic and eternal, spanning all time and space.	
Confronts	Prideful rebellion against the righteous rule of God—the core of human iniquity.	Human bondage to evil, sin, and death.

Parameter	Gospel of the Kingdom of God	Gospel of God
Focus	Jesus Christ as King of kings and Lord of lords as presented in the Synoptic Gospels (Matthew, Mark and Luke) and the Book of Acts.	The atoning death, burial, and resurrection of Jesus Christ, which makes possible God's gracious gifts of righteousness, regeneration, sanctification, and glorification.
Response	**Repent and believe** (Mark 1:14-15) by turning from prideful rebellion with wholehearted repentance and submitting to Christ's kingly rule.	**Confess, receive, and believe** (John 1:10-13 & Romans 10:9) by wholeheartedly embracing Jesus Christ as both Savior and Lord.
Perversion	Legalism (too much law)	Antinomianism (no law)

Q 8.   Reflecting again on the two columns of this table, discuss your strategy for embracing both the gospel of the kingdom of God and the gospel of God in a balanced way, and thereby avoiding the extremes of either legalism or antinomianism.

Notes & Reflections

Session 9. Review & Discussion

As we consider the scope and richness of the Christian gospel message, including its revelation of God's holiness, justice, and unspeakable grace, we are filled with awe and amazement. To think that the God of the universe would have in mind a means to resolve the issue of evil, sin, and death through the sacrificial offering of His very own Son, the second Person of the Godhead, is more than our feeble minds can grasp. Why would a holy God sacrifice Himself to save sinful people such as we are? It is humbling beyond belief.

Yet, the God who created the universe and all that is in it knows our frame – that we are but dust and by nature sinful – and He sacrificed Himself on our behalf that we might have life. All He requires is that we sincerely repent of our prideful rebellion against Him (living our lives as if He doesn't exist), submit to His righteous rule, and receive by faith the salvation which Jesus Christ purchased for us at such a horrendous cost.

He draws us to Himself, yet we make the decision to receive His grace. However, our faith response to the gospel is in nowise meritorious. Indeed, we are saved by grace through faith, and this is not our own doing; it is the gift of God, and not of works so no one can boast. For we are His workmanship, created in Christ Jesus unto good works, that God has prepared ahead of time that we should walk in them (Ephesians 2:8-10). By means of the gospel, He makes us to be citizens of His kingdom and members of His household, destined to live eternally under His gracious rule and to serve Him unreservedly.

Take a few moments to reflect upon the eternal scope and magnitude of the gospel and offer your sacrifice of praise and worship to the Lord.

Q 1.   In what ways did this book increase your understanding of the gospel?

Q 2.   Why is it important to present a holistic, balanced view of the gospel?

Q 3.   How can you guard against perversions such as antinomianism and legalism?

Understanding and giving mental assent to the gospel message is necessary, but it is not sufficient for salvation. The presence of the kind of faith that brings salvation gives rise to a desire to obey and practice the gospel. In this regard, the final phrase of the fourth verse of the hymn *When I Survey the Wondrous Cross* affirms the following:

> ... Love so amazing, so divine, demands my soul, my life, my all.

Early in my Christian experience, I was taught that the more appropriate ending of this hymn would affirm the following:

> ... ***Love so amazing, so divine, shall have my soul, my life, my all.***

Indeed, this is the cry of the heart that has been delivered from eternal death into eternal life.

In view of the infinite sacrifice that Jesus Christ, the Son of God, has made to effect this deliverance, it is only appropriate that I should reckon that all that I am and have belongs to Him, to be consumed for His glory and for the advancement of His kingdom.

Obedience to the gospel entails a lifelong project of cooperating with the Holy Spirit in His work of reproducing the heart of Jesus Christ inside my skin.

This lifelong project is what we designate as **sanctification** – the making holy of that which was previously unclean. As the sanctification process unfolds, our personalities are transformed so as to increasingly reflect the glorious personality of Jesus Christ. For some, like the Apostle Paul, the transformation is radical and abrupt, while for others, like the Apostle Peter, it is a more gradual process with ebbs and flows. Regardless of the trajectory of the sanctification process, our personalities should place in evidence the glory of Christ, drawing people to us to ask us about the hope that we have in Him.

Q 4.   In what ways has this study contributed to your ability to answer questions about the hope that you have in Christ?

Q 5.   Compile a list of Scripture verses or passages you might use in sharing the message of the gospel. Be sure to include both aspects of the gospel.

Q 6.   Write out your testimony as you would share it with a family member, friend, neighbor, or work associate. Then share it with your discussion group.

Notes & Reflections

Afterword

About Us

WitW is a product of Daystar Institute of Biblical Theology and Leadership Development (DI), which is dedicated to supporting local churches in fulfillment of their mission of making disciples of all nations. We have two offices: DI / NM is based in Albuquerque, New Mexico, and DI / A is based in Kampala, Uganda. Please do not hesitate to contact us at www.DaystarInstitute/NM.us if you have any questions or comments or wish to request training in the use of our materials.

Peter Briggs is founder and president-emeritus of Daystar Institute of Biblical Theology & Leadership Development. In addition to teaching and mentoring, Dr. Briggs has authored the WitW Study Guide Series to challenge students in uncompromising discipleship, practical Christian theology, and building a biblical worldview. The WitW study has had a great impact in both East Africa and the USA and is an excellent tool for encouraging and equipping disciples of Jesus to actually live out their faith.

Dedication

The *Walking in the Way of Christ & the Apostles Study Guide Series* is dedicated to Reverend Morris Wanje, whose prayers for God to raise up a means for strengthening and equipping young pastors and church leaders in East Africa caused the Holy Spirit of God to move upon the hearts of godly men and women at Daystar Institute/NM to create this study.

71

Acknowledgments

I am grateful for the heroic efforts of our team of contributors, editors, board of directors, and all who have had a part in the development of the WitW study. In particular, I extend my heartfelt gratitude to my wife, Rosemarie, our daughter, Ruthanne Hamrick, and ministry associates John & Marcie Kinzer, Stephen Patterson, and Michael & Antoninah Mutinda, for their valuable input and help with the Study Guide Series; and to Darienne Dumas and Emily Fuller for proof-reading the texts.

Testimonials

"The *Walking in the Way of Christ & the Apostles* (WitW) series by Dr. Peter Briggs is a powerful tool for fulfilling Jesus' universal mandate to make disciples. WitW is theologically sound, conceptually brilliant, and life- changing for those who are trained by it. The impact of WitW is not only personal transformation into the image of Christ, but also a profound influence on families, churches, and the larger culture, whether in America or Africa or anywhere else. Peter Briggs is a theologian of substantial import, but he has not merely plied his theological craft in the halls of academia. With God's enablement, he has managed to translate biblical truth and disciple-making principles into something that actually works in the real world! Those who embrace and employ *Walking in the Way* in their own lives will find themselves part of a movement affecting generations to come."

Steven Collins, PhD, Executive Dean, Trinity Southwest University

"*Walking in the Way of Christ & the Apostles* (WitW) is a magnificent literary work in biblical theology that offers the student an education in practical Christianity. The WitW study was first introduced in November 2011; since that time we have been using it to instruct ministry leaders and rural pastors at a low cost, and the transformation of lives is phenomenal. Learners get to understand the message of the Bible and are able to study it effectively. In my own interaction with the material since 2012, I have come to realize that Jesus Christ is using it to revive His remnant in Kenya and other parts of Africa, teaching us how to think in a biblical way and be successful in all spheres of life. I am convinced that the WitW material holds the key to Africa's revival, and, in Yahweh's hand, it is a mighty tool for returning the continent back to Him."

Michael Mutinda, Team Leader, Daystar Institute / Africa

Walking in the Way of Christ & the Apostles
Study Guide Series

Part 1: Foundational Principles. These principles are foundational to equip the Christ-follower to have and to be governed by the mind of Christ.

1. The Way of God
2. The Storyline of the Bible
3. Biblical Reality
4. Discovering the Meaning of Scripture
5. Torah: The Fountainhead of Wisdom
6. The Two-Part Christian Gospel

Part 2: The Gospel of the Kingdom of God. Here we explore the ways in which the Christian gospel confronts the prideful rebellion of the human heart and exalts Christ as King over all.

7. Authority of the King
8. Called by the King
9. The Meaning of Discipleship
10. Disciplines of the Kingdom
11. Household of the King
12. The Second Coming of the King

Part 3 – The Gospel of God. This final set explores how the Christian gospel affords a complete solution to human depravity and the threefold problem of sin and death.

13. Introduction to the Gospel of God
14. The Reason for the Gospel of God
15. Content of the Gospel of God
16. Perversions of the Gospel of God
17. Application of the Gospel of God

Theological Readers (TR)

TR1 – Part 1: Foundational Principles
TR2 – Part 2: The Gospel of the Kingdom of God
TR3 – Part 3: The Gospel of God
TR4 – Resources and Appendices

Theological Handbooks (TH)

TH1 – Part 1: The Way of God
TH2 – Part 2
TH3 – Part 3

Connect with us at www.DaystarInstituteNM.us, or
Contact us via email at WalkingintheWayUSA@gmail.com

www.ingramcontent.com/pod-product-compliance
Lightning Source LLC
Chambersburg PA
CBHW071928020426
42331CB00010B/2767